nabokov Bush Theatre

nabokov and the Bush Theatre in association with
Watford Palace Theatre and Mercury Theatre Colchester present

2nd May 1997

by Jack Thorne

8 September – 10 October 2009

2nd May 1997 on tour

20 – 21 October   Watford Palace Theatre
22 – 24 October   Mercury Theatre, Colchester
27 – 31 October   The Studio, Royal Exchange Theatre, Manchester

Cast and Creative Team

Jake	**James Barrett**
Robert	**Geoffrey Beevers**
Marie	**Linda Broughton**
Will	**Jamie Samuel**
Ian	**Hugh Skinner**
Sarah	**Phoebe Waller-Bridge**
Writer	**Jack Thorne**
Director	**George Perrin**
Designer	**Hannah Clark**
Lighting Designer	**Philip Gladwell**
Sound Designer	**Emma Laxton**
Assistant Director	**Joe Murphy**
Movement Director	**Kate Sagovsky**
Assistant Lighting Designer / Tour Relighter	**Anna Eveleigh**
Production Manager	**Dave Agnew**
Company Stage Manager	**Nick Hayman**
Assistant Stage Manager	**Jessica Harwood**
Scenery Construction	**George Orange** **Mark Tweed**

The Bush Theatre would like to give particular thanks to: aka, West 12 Shopping Centre, Westfield London and the John Thaw Foundation.

nabokov would like to give particular thanks to: Dr Nick Allen, Hazel Blears, Rose Cobbe, Dee Evans, Harry Hepple, Brigid Larmour, Roger McCann, Josie Rourke, Jeremy Sharpe and Penelope Skinner.

nabokov and the Bush would like to thank: 354 Print Ltd, English National Opera, Harmsworth Printing Ltd, London Academy of Music and Dramatic Art, Queen's Theatre Hornchurch, Royal Academy of Dramatic Art, Joe Schermoly and Stage Technologies.

2nd May 1997 received its world premiere on 8 September 2009.

James Barrett Jake

James trained at the Manchester School of Acting.

Theatre includes: *Key to a Quiet Life* (Dead Earnest Theatre).

TV includes: *Doctors, Literacy Awareness*.

Film includes: *Kiss, Cuddle, Torture*.

Geoffrey Beevers Robert

Theatre includes: *The UN Inspector, Playing With Fire, The Winter's Tale* (National Theatre); *War and Peace, Passage to India* (Shared Experience); *A Servant to Two Masters, Pericles, The Comedy of Errors, Henry VIII, The Devils, The Time of Your Life* (RSC); *Hamlet, The Antipodes* (Shakespeare's Globe); *Leaving, The Skin Game, Dr Knock, Uncle Vanya* (Orange Tree); *The Robbers* (Gate); *The Tower* (Almeida); *Twelfth Night* (English Touring Theatre); *Romeo and Juliet, The Crucible* (Young Vic); and several plays in the West End.

TV includes: *The Tudors, The South Bank Show on Hardy, Thatcher: The Long Walk to Finchley, The Genius of Mozart, Island at War, Goodnight Mr Tom, Silent Witness, Inspector Morse, Sherlock Holmes, Poirot, Holby City, Casualty, The Bill, Down to Earth, Taggart, Buddha of Suburbia, Prime Suspect, Red Dwarf, Yes Prime Minister, A Very Peculiar Practice, Dr Who, A Very British Coup, Jewel in the Crown*.

Film includes: *Clash of the Titans, The Kid, Miss Potter, The Edge of Love, The Woodlanders, The Curse of the Pink Panther, Victor/Victoria*.

Geoffrey also writes and directs. His adaptation of *Adam Bede* won a Time Out Award.

Linda Broughton Marie

Theatre includes: *Ivanov* (Wyndham's Theatre); *The Chalk Garden* (Donmar Warehouse); *Snowbound* (Trafalgar Studios); *Hamlet* (The Factory); *I Like Mine with a Kiss* (Bush); *The Safari Party* (New Vic, Stoke); *Hoxton Story* (Red Room); *The Life of Galileo, The Crucible, Racing Demon, Absence of War, Murmuring Judges* (Birmingham Rep); *Ballroom* (Riverside Studios and tour); *The Importance of Being Earnest* (Northampton Theatre Royal); *When the Wind Blows* (Southwark Playhouse); *Northanger Abbey, Forty Years On* (Northcott, Exeter); *Sugar Dollies* (Gate).

TV includes: *Waking The Dead, Silent Witness, Doctors, Poirot, Carrie and Barrie, Fist of Fun, Paul Merton: Does China Exist?, Casualty, Roughnecks, Knowing Me Knowing You, Chandler and Co, Men Behaving Badly, Wycliffe, Firm Friends, Hetty Wainthropp Investigates, Coronation Street.*

Film includes: *Babel, Bridget Jones's Diary, Sliding Doors, Watch That Man.*

In the 1970s Linda was one of the founding members of Monstrous Regiment. She is currently a member of The Factory.

Jamie Samuel Will

Jamie trained at Arts Educational School of Acting.

Theatre includes: *The English Game* (Headlong); *The Conservatory* (Old Red Lion); *Gormenghast, Nana, A Midsummer Night's Dream, Jekyll and Hyde, Romeo and Juliet, The Lover, Lady Windermere's Fan, Once in a Lifetime, Metamorphosis, Three Sisters, Someone Who'll Watch Over Me* (ArtsEd).

TV includes: *A Touch of Frost, The Bill, Doctors.*

Hugh Skinner Ian

Hugh trained at LAMDA.

Theatre includes: *suddenlossofdignity.com* (Bush); *The Great Game* (Tricycle); *Angry Young Man* (Trafalgar Studios); *The Enchantment* (National Theatre); *Senora Carrar's Rifles* (Young Vic); *French Without Tears* (English Touring Theatre); *Savage/Love* (Theatre503).

TV includes: *Tess of the D'Urbervilles, Bonkers.*

Film includes: *Day of the Dead.*

Phoebe Waller-Bridge Sarah

Phoebe trained at RADA.

Theatre includes: *Roaring Trade* (Soho); *Twelfth Night* (Sprite Productions); *Crazy Love* (Paines Plough); *Is Everyone OK?* (nabokov theatre company).

TV includes: *Doctors.*

Film includes: *Lost Hearts, Intangible, The Reward.*

Phoebe is Co-Artistic Director of DryWrite (www.drywrite.com).

Hannah Clark Designer

Hannah trained in theatre design at Nottingham Trent University and Central School of Speech and Drama. She was a winner of the 2005 Linbury Biennial Prize for stage design.

Theatre includes: *A Midsummer Night's Dream* (Shakespeare's Globe); *Thyestes, Torn* (Arcola); *Under Milk Wood* (Northampton Theatre Royal); *Nocturnal, Big Love* (Gate, London); *Billy Wonderful* (Liverpool Everyman); *Hortensia and the Museum of Dreams* (Vanbrugh Theatre, RADA); *The Snow Queen* (West Yorkshire Playhouse); *Proper Clever* (Liverpool Playhouse); *Pequenas Delicias* (Requardt & Company); *Roadkill Café* (Requardt & Company, Centro Coreográfico De Montemor-O-Novo, Portugal/Teatro Fondamenta Nuove, Venice/The Place); *House of Agnes* (Paines Plough); *Breakfast With Mugabe* (Theatre Royal Bath); *The Cracks in My Skin, Who's Afraid of Virginia Woolf?* (Manchester Royal Exchange); *Othello* (Salisbury Playhouse); *As You Like It, We That Are Left* (Watford Palace Theatre); *Terre Haute* (Assembly Rooms, Edinburgh/Trafalgar Studios/UK tour/59e59, New York); *The Taming of the Shrew* (Bristol Old Vic); *Jammy Dodgers* (Requardt & Company, The Place/Royal Opera House 2/international tour); *Death of a Salesman, What the Butler Saw, Blue/Orange, A View from the Bridge, I Just Stopped By To See the Man, Two, Frankie and Johnny in the Clair De Lune* (Bolton Octagon).

Anna Eveleigh Assistant Lighting Designer / Tour Relighter

Anna is currently studying at the Royal Welsh College of Music and Drama.

Theatre includes: *In My Mouth* (RWCMD/Piccolo Theatre); *The Speculator* (RWCMD).

Philip Gladwell Lighting Designer

Theatre includes: *Punk Rock* (Lyric Hammersmith/Royal Exchange Manchester); *Origins* (Pentabus); *Terminus* (Abbey and tour); *Once on this Island* (Birmingham/Nottingham/Hackney); *After Dido* (English National Opera); *Macbeth* (Royal Exchange Manchester); *Harvest* (UK tour); *Amazonia, Ghosts, The Member of the Wedding, Festa!* (Young Vic); *Oedipus Rex* (Royal Festival Hall); *Oxford Street, Kebab* (Royal Court); *Il Trittico* (Opera Zuid); *Testing the Echo* (Out of Joint); *Falstaff* (Grange Park Opera); *Blithe Spirit, Black Comedy* (Watermill); *Drowning On Dry Land* (Salisbury Playhouse); *Overspill, HOTBOI, Tape* (Soho); *Melody, In the Bag* (Traverse, Edinburgh); *Mother Courage* (Nottingham Playhouse/UK tour); *Into the Woods, Macbeth, Way Up Stream* (Derby Playhouse); *The Bodies* (Live Theatre); *The Morris* (Liverpool Everyman); *Bread and Butter* (Tricycle); *Canterville Ghost* (Peacock); *Awakening, Another America* (Sadler's Wells).

Emma Laxton Sound Designer

Theatre at the Bush includes: *Apologia, The Contingency Plan, Wrecks, Broken Space Season, 2000 Feet Away, Tinderbox.*

West End theatre includes: *Treasure Island* (Theatre Royal Haymarket); *That Face* (Duke Of York's); *My Name Is Rachel Corrie* (Playhouse Theatre).

Theatre for the Royal Court includes: *Tusk Tusk, Faces in the Crowd, That Face, Gone Too Far!, Catch, Scenes From The Back of Beyond, Woman and Scarecrow, The World's Biggest Diamond, Incomplete And Random Acts of Kindness, My Name Is Rachel Corrie* (also Minetta Lane, New York/Galway Festival/ Edinburgh Festival), *Bone, The Weather, Bear Hug, Terrorism, Food Chain.*

Other theatre includes: *Ghosts* (ATC at Arcola); *Pornography* (Tricycle/Birmingham Rep/Traverse, Edinburgh); *A Christmas Carol* (Chichester); *Welcome to Ramallah* (iceandfire); *Shoot/Get Treasure/Repeat* (National Theatre); *Europe* (Dundee Rep/Barbican Pit); *Other Hands* (Soho); *The Unthinkable* (Sheffield Theatres); *My Dad is a Birdman* (Young Vic); *The Gods are Not to Blame* (Tiata Fahodzi at Arcola).

Joe Murphy Assistant Director

Joe has a BA (Hons) in Drama from Exeter University, and a PG Dip in Theatre Directing from Mountview Academy of Performing Arts.

Theatre as Director includes: *Service, Building Site* (Arcola/Miniaturists); *After, Come On Over* (Tristan Bates); *The Things that Never Grew in the Garden* (Hampstead Start Night); *Normal* (Cockpit); *Julius Caesar, Esme-Tales* (Edinburgh Fringe).

Theatre as Assistant Director includes: *Fixer* (High Tide Festival); *Purgatory* (Arcola); *Girls and Dolls* (Old Red Lion); *He Said...* (Bush).

George Perrin Director

Co-founder and Artistic Director of nabokov and Creative Associate at the Bush Theatre.

Directing work at the Bush includes: *Sea Wall.*

Other theatre as Director includes: *Is Everyone Ok?* (Latitude Festival and national tour, nabokov); *House of Agnes* (Oval House, Paines Plough); *The Dirt Under the Carpet, Crazy Love* (Òran Mór, Glasgow/Shunt Vaults London/Paines Plough); *Terre Haute* (Assembly Rooms, Edinburgh/Trafalgar Studios/UK tour/59e59, New York); *My Little Heart Dropped in Coffee, Babies* (Paines Plough/Young Vic Wild Lunch); *Camarilla* (Old Red Lion/nabokov).

Theatre as Associate Director includes: *Long Time Dead* (Drum Theatre Plymouth/Paines Plough); *After the End* (New York/Moscow/national tour/Paines Plough); *Nikolina* (nabokov national tour). He was Trainee Associate Director of Paines Plough and Watford Palace Theatre.

He was the first recipient of the Genesis Director's Award from the Young Vic and is a member of Old Vic New Voices. George trained on the National Theatre Studio Directors' Course and at the Maly Theatre, St Petersburg with the Young Vic.

Kate Sagovsky Movement Director

Kate trained in Dance Studies at Laban after completing an MA in Movement Studies at the Central School of Speech and Drama and a BA in English at Oxford University.

Work as Movement Director includes: *The Unspeakable* (Tristan Bates); *Chauntecleer and Pertelotte* (Hen and Chickens/Old Red Lion/Brighton Fringe/Edinburgh Fringe); *Flesh* (Urban Exchange tour: Westminster Abbey, London and St John's, Edinburgh); *The Wedding Party*, *Semi-Monde* (Embassy); *Les Liaisons Dangereuses* (Greenwich); *Cyrano De Bergerac*, *Trojan Women* (Oxford Playhouse).

Kate also directs physical/dance theatre, including: *Half Man/Half Clam* (Create Festival 09, Arcola); *Towards the Void* (Bonnie Bird); *Chinese Takeaway* (The Accidental Festival, ICA); *Not For Sale* (Freefall/CHASTE tour: Camden People's Theatre, London, and Pleasance Courtyard, Edinburgh).

Jack Thorne Writer

Writing for theatre includes: *When You Cure Me* (Bush), *Stacy* (Arcola and Trafalgar Studios), *Fanny and Faggot* (Finborough and Trafalgar Studios) and *Burying Your Brother in the Pavement* (NT Connections).

Writing for television includes: episodes of *Skins*, *Shameless*, and the upcoming *Cast-Offs* (Channel 4, co-written with Tony Roche and Alex Bulmer) and *This is England* (Channel 4, co-written with Shane Meadows).

Writing for radio includes: *When You Cure Me, People Snogging in Public Places* (Radio 3); *Left at the Angel* (Radio 4); an adaptation of *The Hunchback of Notre Dame* (with Alex Bulmer, Radio 4).

His first feature film *The Scouting Book for Boys* (Celador Films/Film4/ Screen East) will open at the San Sebastian International Film Festival in September and has its UK premiere at The Times BFI London Film Festival in October.

The Bush Theatre

'One of the most experienced prospectors of raw talent in Europe'
The Independent

For thirty-seven years, the Bush Theatre has pursued its singular vision of discovery, risk and entertainment from its home in Shepherds Bush. That vision is valued and embraced by a community of audience and artists radiating out from our distinctive corner of West London across the world. The Bush is a local theatre with an international reputation. Since its inception, the Bush has produced hundreds of groundbreaking premieres, many of them Bush commissions, and hosted guest productions by leading companies and artists from across the world. On any given night, those queuing at the foot of our stairs to take their seats could have travelled from Auckland or popped in from round the corner.

What draws them to the Bush is the promise of a good night out and our proven commitment to launch, from our stage, successive generations of playwrights and artists. Samuel Adamson, David Eldridge, Jonathan Harvey, Catherine Johnson, Tony Kushner, Stephen Poliakoff, Jack Thorne and Victoria Wood (all then unknown) began their careers at the Bush. The unwritten contract between talent and risk is understood by actors who work at the Bush, creating roles in untested new plays. Unique amongst local theatres, the Bush consistently draws actors of the highest reputation and calibre. Joseph Fiennes and Ian Hart recently took leading roles in a first play by an unknown playwright to great critical success. John Simm and Richard Wilson acted in premieres both of which transferred into the West End. The Bush has won over 100 awards, and developed an enviable reputation for touring its acclaimed productions nationally and internationally.

Audiences and organisations far beyond our stage profit from the risks we take. The value attached to the Bush by other theatres and by the film and television industries is both significant and considerable. The Bush receives more than 1,000 scripts through the post every year, and reads and responds to them all. This is one small part of a comprehensive playwrights' development programme which nurtures the relationship between writer and director, as well as playwright residencies and commissions. Everything that we do to develop playwrights focuses them towards a production on our stage or beyond.

We have also launched an ambitious new education, training and professional development programme, **bush**futures, providing opportunities for different sectors of the community and professionals to access the expertise of Bush playwrights, directors, designers, technicians and actors, and to play an active role in influencing the future development of the theatre and its programme. Over the next three years we aim to increase the reach and impact of the work we do by seeking out and developing networks for writers using digital technology and the internet. Through this pioneering work, the Bush will reach and connect with new writers and new audiences.

Josie Rourke
Artistic Director

At the Bush Theatre

Artistic Director	**Josie Rourke**
Executive Director	**Angela Bond**
Associate Director **bush**futures	**Anthea Williams**
Associate Director	**James Grieve**
Finance Manager	**Viren Thakker**
Marketing Manager	**Stephanie Hui**
Production Manager	**Anthony Newton**
Company Stage Manager	**Angela Riddell**
Producers	**Caroline Dyott** **Tara Wilkinson**
Developement Manager	**Kirsty Raper**
Developement Officers	**Bethany Ann McDonald** **Leonora Twynam**
Box Office & Front of House Manager	**Clare Moss**
Box Office Assistants	**Kirsty Cox, Asha Jennings Grant,** **Alex Hern, Ava Leman Morgan,** **Lee Maxwell Simpson**
Front of House Duty Managers	**Kellie Batchelor, Rachael Boulton,** **Euan Forsyth, Alex Hern, Kate McGregor,** **Ava Leman Morgan, Sam Plumb,** **Rose Romain, Lois Tucker**
Duty Technicians	**Dave Blakemore, Viv Clavering, Deb Jones,** **Sara Macleod, Ben Sherratt, Kris Snaddon,** **Matthew Vile**
Associate Artists	**Tanya Burns, Arthur Darvill,** **Chloe Emmerson, James Farncombe,** **Richard Jordan, Emma Laxton,** **Paul Miller, Lucy Osborne**
Associate Playwright	**Anthony Weigh**
Creative Associates	**Nathan Curry, Charlotte Gwinner,** **Clare Lizzimore, George Perrin,** **Hamish Pirie, Lyndsey Turner,** **Richard Twyman, Dawn Walton**
Writer in Residence	**Jack Thorne**
Press Representative	**Ewan Thomson**
Resident Assistant Director	**Ant Stones**
Intern	**Pippa Howie**

The Bush Theatre
Shepherds Bush Green
London W12 8QD

Box Office: 020 8743 5050
www.bushtheatre.co.uk

The Alternative Theatre Company Ltd. (The Bush Theatre)
is a Registered Charity number: 270080
Co. registration number 1221968 | VAT no. 228 3163 73

Supported by
ARTS COUNCIL ENGLAND

Be there at the beginning

Our work identifying and nurturing playwrights is only made possible through the generous support of our Patrons and other donors. Thank you to all those who have supported us during the last year.

If you are interested in finding out how to be involved, please visit the 'Support Us' section of www.bushtheatre.co.uk, or call 020 8743 3584.

Lone Star
Eric Abraham & Sigrid Rausing
Gianni Alen-Buckley
Catherine Johnson

Handful of Stars
Anonymous
Jim Broadbent
Clyde Cooper
David and Alexander Emmerson
Tom Erhardt
Julia Foster
Albert and Lyn Fuss
David and Anita Miles
Richard and Elizabeth Phillips
Alan Rickman
Paul and Jill Ruddock
Susie Sainsbury
John and Tita Shakeshaft
Charles Wansbrough

Glee Club
Anonymous
John Botrill
Alan Brodie
David Brooks
Maggie Burrows
Clive Butler
Vivien Goodwin
Sheila Hancock
Virginia Ironside
Adam Kenwright
Neil LaBute
Antonia Lloyd
Kirsty Mclaren
Michael McCoy
Judith Mellor
John and Jacqui Pearson
Mr and Mrs A Radcliffe
John Reynolds
Brian D Smith
Abigail Uden

Bush Club
Anonymous
Nic Arnold
Mr and Mrs Badrichani
Veronica Baxter
Geraldine Caulfield
Kay Ellen Consolver
Sarah Crowley
Matthew Cushen
Joy Dean
Camilla Emson
Karen Germain
Carol Ann Gill
Sally Godley
Miranda Greig
Jenny Hall
Sian Hansen
Andy Herrity
Mr G Hopkinson
Rebecca Hornby
Mrs M J Patricia Jacobson
Hardeep Kalsi
Robin Kermode
Vincent Luck
Ray Miles
Toby Moorcroft - Sayle Screen
Mr and Mrs Ogden
Andrew Peck
Julian and Amanda Platt
Radfin Courier Service
Radfin Antiques
Volinka Reina
Clare Rich
Mark Roberts
Martin Shenfield
Johanna Schmitz
Anne Taylor
Solvene Tiffou
John and Joanna Trotter
Francois Von Hurter
Geoffrey Whight
Alison Winter

Corporate Sponsors
Anonymous
The Agency (London) Ltd
Harbottle & Lewis LLP
Ludgate Environmental Ltd
Curtis Brown Group Ltd
Orion Management
West12 Shopping & Leisure Centre
Westfield London

Trusts and Foundations
The John S Cohen Foundation
The Daisy Trust
The D'Oyly Carte Charitable Trust
The Earls Court & Olympia Charitable Trust
The Elizabeth & Gordon Bloor Charitable Foundation
The Ernest Cook Trust
Garfield Weston Foundation
The Gatsby Charitable Foundation
The Girdlers' Company Charitable Trust
Haberdashers' Benevolent Foundation
Jerwood Charitable Foundation
The John Thaw Foundation
The Kobler Trust
The Laurie & Gillian Marsh Charitable Trust
The Marina Kleinwort Trust
The Martin Bowley Charitable Trust
Old Possum's Practical Trust
The Thistle Trust
The Vandervell Foundation
The Harold Hyam Wingate Foundation
The Peggy Ramsay Foundation
The Peter Wolff Theatre Trust

nabokov

'Proving that political drama does have a place in the 21st Century'
The List

nabokov is a new-writing theatre company dedicated to commissioning, developing and producing backlash theatre – new work that offers an antagonistic response to contemporary agendas, trends and events. The company tours nationally and internationally with a commitment to the Eastern Region, where the company is based.

Since 2001, we have produced critically acclaimed productions in London, Edinburgh and on tour including *Kitchen*, *Bedtime for Bastards*, *Camarilla* and *Nikolina*. Our world premiere production of *Artefacts* by Mike Bartlett opened at the Bush Theatre in London before touring nationally and transferring to New York. *Terre Haute* by Edmund White premiered at the Assembly Rooms, Edinburgh, prior to a National Tour and runs in the West End and Off-Broadway.

Our PRESENT:TENSE events challenge playwrights to write plays in response to the most important story on the news agenda. Our multi-arts event the NABOKOV ARTS CLUB features plays, performance poetry, films, comedy, live music and DJs. Alongside our own events and productions, nabokov curates, produces and hosts work at festivals and events including the Latitude Festival and the Innocent Village Fete.

For **nabokov**

Artistic Directors	**James Grieve** and **George Perrin**
Executive Director	**Ric Mountjoy**
Associate Producers	**Emma Brunjes** and **Imogen Kinchin**
Producer – *2nd May 1997*	**Kate Mackonochie**
Assistant Producer – *2nd May 1997*	**Marlaina Darmody**
Producer – *Is Everyone OK?*	**Suzanne Carter**
Producer – *Every Brilliant Thing*	**Davina Shah**
Office and Project Assistants	**Anningwaa Boakye-Yiadom** and **Hannah Scott**
Literary Assistant	**Georgia Gatti**
Playwright-In-Residence	**Joel Horwood**

Contact us:
hello@nabokov-online.com

Visit our website:
www.nabokov-online.com

LOTTERY FUNDED

Watford Palace Theatre

This is an exciting time at Watford Palace Theatre. WPT aims to be the creative centre at the heart of Watford, engaging with all the communities of Watford, Hertfordshire and the surrounding region. It creates live and interactive experiences that are inclusive, uplifting and empowering whilst developing a national and international reputation for exceptional and diverse theatre.

Watford has a population of just over 80,000, of whom around twenty per cent (including forty per cent school-age students) are from minority ethnic backgrounds. The Palace is a 600-seat producing venue (one of three producing theatres in the region, the others being in Colchester and Ipswich), and receives revenue funding from Arts Council England East and Watford Borough Council. The annual programme consists of in-house productions and co-productions, presenting touring productions and a programme of participatory activities that together attract the widest possible local audiences. The theatre was originally built as a music hall, and celebrated its Centenary in 2008.

The Mercury Theatre, Colchester

The Mercury Theatre is a highly respected regional theatre and home to the critically acclaimed Mercury Theatre Company, staging a broad mix of classic plays and new writing as well as working extensively within the local community. It has been successful since its inception in 1999, being described by the *Daily Telegraph* as 'a hive of artistic excellence' and by the *Guardian* as 'one of the best small reps in the country.' It is a venue for the best touring theatre and entertainment as well as providing a platform for local performing arts groups and artists.

Since 2003, the Company has built up a strong reputation and audience for new writing. Amongst others, the Mercury collaborates with Dialogue Productions, Real Circumstance, Tilted Productions, The New Wolsey Theatre, Wildworks, Scamp Theatre and is delighted to be working with nabokov, the Bush Theatre and Watford Palace Theatre for this production of *2nd May 1997*. To find out more about the Mercury Theatre Colchester please visit www.mercurytheatre.co.uk

ALSO AT THE BUSH THIS SEASON...

BY NICK PAYNE
17 OCT–21 NOV

DIRECTION JOSIE ROURKE **DESIGN** LUCY OSBORNE
LIGHTING OLIVER FENWICK **SOUND** EMMA LAXTON

THE STEFAN GOLASZEWSKI PLAYS

BY STEFAN GOLASZEWSKI
2 DEC–9 JAN

DIRECTION & DESIGN PHILLIP BREEN **CAST** STEFAN GOLASZEWSKI

THE WHISKY TASTER

BY JAMES GRAHAM
20 JAN–20 FEB

DIRECTION JAMES GRIEVE **DESIGN** LUCY OSBORNE **LIGHTING** JAMES FARNCOMBE

BY PENELOPE SKINNER
EIGENGRAU
10 MAR–10 APR

[ay-gen-gr-ow] -noun intrinsic light;
the colour seen by the eye in perfect darkness

DIRECTION POLLY FINDLAY **DESIGN** HANNAH CLARK **LIGHTING** MATTHEW PITMAN

Mon – Sat 7.30pm, matinees 2.30pm
Tickets £15 (£13 concessions)
Box Office 020 8743 5050
www.bushtheatre.co.uk

bush theatre

2ND MAY 1997

Jack Thorne

For Laura Wade

'What the electorate gives, the electorate can take away'

Tony Blair

Characters

ROBERT, *seventy-one*
MARIE, *sixty-four*
SARAH, *twenty-eight*
IAN, *twenty-nine*
JAKE, *eighteen*
WILL, *eighteen*

This text went to press before the end of rehearsals and so may differ slightly from the play as performed.

PART ONE

11.38 p.m.

The simple yet textured bedroom of a cultured older couple.

ROBERT *sits up in a slightly grand bed, looking at a small packet of photos; seventy-ish and handsome, he is wearing reading glasses. There is an oxygen cylinder beside his bed. He's calling offstage.*

ROBERT. So which one's this and why's she in a bikini?

He flicks to another photo.

And this one – this one's new. I recognise him. But I don't know where from. He's not the new one, is he?

He continues to flick.

MARIE (*from off*). No. The new one wasn't with her. They were all just friends...

ROBERT. They seem to have – well, he's certainly touching her, not – I'm never sure what touching is friendly any more. But that I wouldn't say was...

If I'd have touched Mary Watson like that, I'd have been slapped.

MARIE *is in the ensuite bathroom. She is making quite a lot of noise in there, working her new electric toothbrush.*

MARIE (*she stays off*). Mary Watson?

ROBERT. Mary? I must have told you. Mary? First – well, first something. She let me hold hands with her once, and then said I was too clammy – said my hands felt like goose grease. I realised then – if she could afford goose in her house – well, no chance for me. I don't know why I'm remembering her.

Mary? Do I mean Mary Watson? Maybe it was Phillips. You'd remember her name better than I, and I'd have surely told you… Maybe it wasn't Mary.

Do you hear that? The bells of Alzheimer's. The bells. The bells. Remembering –

Bikini.

Bikini.

MARIE. You do not have Alzheimer's…

ROBERT. There's about twenty shots of this girl in a bikini. Same – bikini – well, some – no, same bikini, just different angle. More of a – bottom one –

Bikini.

Bikini.

MARIE. She's just trying to keep us involved, darling…

ROBERT. Funny way to stay involved, to show us lots of shots of this girl's bottom.

He turns a photo through ninety degrees in his hands – he raises his eyebrow in surprise.

MARIE. She thought we'd want to see them.

ROBERT. But they're not of anything, well, not of –

MARIE. Then put them back in the envelope and finish your speech.

He thinks, and then continues flicking through.

ROBERT. A few landscapes. A spot of nature wouldn't be… People on a beach in their pants – touching each other… and 'clubbing'. There are some of 'clubbing'. Did I tell you about the 'clubbing ones'? Most of them seem to be wearing bikinis in those too – bikinis and sunglasses indoors.

MARIE. It was a holiday, Robert. Not a fact-finding mission.

ROBERT. Oh. Yes. Not that – facts. I firmly disagree with the notion that facts and entertainment are somehow different entities.

He turns over to another picture.

Tweedledum and Tweedledee called from the office.

MARIE. What did they want?

ROBERT. And they're hideously small. These photos.

MARIE. You buy an extra packet for a pound. It's one of those you send off for. But they come in that size.

ROBERT. Well. They're very small.

> MARIE *enters the room and smiles at her husband. She is sixty-ish, stylish, careful; she's wearing a face mask.*

MARIE. Large enough for you to make out a bikini, though…

> ROBERT *looks at her and smiles.*

ROBERT. Yes.

MARIE. Which is surprising because it is not a large bikini.

She smiles and exits for the bathroom again.

He puts down the photos. He picks up a pad and a pen. He looks at them.

ROBERT. They said there's a race on. Tweedlewotsits. The office did. First to declare. Sunderland. Hamilton. Somewhere else. They thought they'd have the first results within the hour.

MARIE (*she stays off*). Maybe we should have the goggleometer on then.

ROBERT. No. No. We'll have quite enough of that later.

He coughs, touches his chest, and then looks around regally. He puts down the pad and the paper with deliberate grace. He thinks for something to do, sighs and picks up the pictures again. He holds them but doesn't look.

Besides, it's Dimbleby versus Dimbleby again tonight. Bored silly with raised eyebrows on one side? Why not change channels and be bored equally silly by the younger and less successful brother? ITV was set up to provide competition, you know.

MARIE. I think he's quite attractive.

ROBERT. David?

MARIE. Jonathan. He has a much kinder face than David. And a slightly grubby smile.

ROBERT. I'd give it to the black man. The – Trevor – you know, the 'And finally…'

MARIE. McDonald.

ROBERT. They said – the office said – 'Nine cabinet members will fall' in their slightly portentous voices…

MARIE. Which one was it? George or…?

ROBERT. You know I don't like it when you call them by their real names…

MARIE. Tweedledum or…?

ROBERT. I have no idea. They're much of a muchness. To be honest with you, there's been once or twice I've almost called them Tweedledum and Tweedledee. 'Nine cabinet members will fall.' No sympathy. Mild excitement in their voices. Moist excitement.

MARIE. Do they know which ones will…?

ROBERT. They said – they told me they wanted to talk to me about 'future opportunities'.

MARIE. I hope you laughed at them.

ROBERT. They've rung about twice during the entire campaign. You don't laugh at crumbs.

MARIE. You *do* laugh at *them*, though.

ROBERT. Norman always thought I'd make a good lord.

MARIE. Norman was flirting with you…

ROBERT *looks off, not exactly surprised at that, but surprised at her tone.*

He turns back to the photos.

ROBERT. Well.

I have no idea who any of them are… in these photos…

MARIE. Hannah's friends.

ROBERT. Yes. I know they're Hannah's friends. But – I'm still not…

MARIE. The girl in the bikini is Kaylee. You know her…

ROBERT. Kaylee? I thought she wore glasses.

He looks more carefully at a photo, he adjusts his own glasses.

MARIE *comes back into the room, the face mask now washed off.*

He smiles at her.

Didn't she – wear glasses…?

She sits on the bed.

She takes the photos from him.

She flicks through and starts pointing out important things.

MARIE. These are the two – Laura and Cherry – she's renting the flat with… and this one's the one who had the problem with the dead dog, Terry –

ROBERT. The one who got her the interview… Well, we like him.

MARIE. And this one's the one who made the silly mistake with the overdose, Kirsty… and this one's that one that wasn't very nice to her, Phil.

ROBERT. Wasn't he?

MARIE. Phil. Second year at Manchester. He told her he loved her, and then found a better bet. When she had the issue with the eating.

He remembers the issue with the eating.

ROBERT. Him?

MARIE. He's nice enough. Just a little confused. Confused Phil.

ROBERT. And why was she on holiday with Confused Phil? Was she confused? He's not the one touching her inappropriately, is he?

MARIE. He's nice enough. Besides, he's in her friendship group, she didn't want to – I think 'alienate' is the word she used.

She smiles at him. He looks at her with a gentle frown.

ROBERT. I didn't think the 'lord' thing was…

She kisses his cheek.

MARIE. I know you didn't.

He pats the bed.

ROBERT. Are you getting in?

MARIE *laughs.*

MARIE. Bikini got your heart racing, is it?

ROBERT *laughs and then coughs.*

ROBERT. No. I didn't mean…

MARIE. No. I know.

MARIE *gets up and opens the wardrobe, she begins to pull out things from inside.*

You tell Tweedledum and Tweedledee that you're very grateful for their interest, but if you're out then you're staying out…

ROBERT *coughs again.*

ROBERT. And shaking it all about.

MARIE. Well, then, tell them what you like…

ROBERT. They're just trying to make the best of a bad egg.

MARIE. They've thrown the bad egg away.

ROBERT *scratches his neck, so as to avoid any telling facial expression.*

ROBERT. Maybe I should take her on holiday…

MARIE. Who?

ROBERT. Hannah. There's plenty she should see. I could show her there's more to life than beaches and 'clubbing'.

MARIE. She's not your next project.

ROBERT. I didn't say that.

MARIE. You could take me on holiday.

ROBERT. I intend to.

ROBERT coughs.

Then coughs again.

Then coughs repeatedly.

Then takes a breath.

MARIE looks at him carefully and turns on the oxygen cylinder.

She gestures the mask towards him.

MARIE. Are you…?

ROBERT pushes the mask away, and opens a drawer and pulls out a clean handkerchief.

He holds it to his mouth as he coughs again.

Then coughs again and again and again.

Then he stops.

He takes the oxygen mask from her and takes two distinct breaths.

Would you like some water?

ROBERT. No.

He checks his handkerchief.

MARIE. Blood?

ROBERT. Only a little.

She exits to the bathroom, pours a glass of water and comes back in with it.

She hands it to him. He takes another two breaths from the mask and takes a sip.

He hands her back the mask, she turns off the oxygen.

MARIE. What has Dr Phillips been saying about…?

ROBERT. He hasn't.

He takes another sip of his water.

They're just trying to support a man who has had his seat taken from him –

MARIE. They're dusting the cornices…

ROBERT. In – well, two hours' time. Three hours' time, I'm out of a job, they're…

MARIE. They don't want you saying anything disrespectful in your speech.

ROBERT *is starting to flush up.*

ROBERT. That's not what – I worked hard for these people, for this Party, a little reward. A – little – reward…

MARIE. If you get worked up like this, you'll start coughing again.

ROBERT. You work me up. You're working me up. They made very clear – compensations would be… They do not call very often, when they do call, it is clear, I should listen to what they have to say, crumbs are… They wanted to talk to me about my future. This is a good thing. Yet, you don't seem…

He coughs.

You don't seem the slightest bit interested. You don't think I should take my daughter away, you don't think –

MARIE. I think you should take me away.

ROBERT *(impassioned). I will not* – simply – *fill* my time.

Beat. MARIE *looks at him, and acknowledges him, like a woman acknowledges a man she loves – but she doesn't concede.*

MARIE. I know you won't.

MARIE *walks over to the wardrobe. She picks out two dresses, and then holds them up against herself.*

This, or this? Hannah says the brown one shows off my figure better.

ROBERT. You wore that to the constituency barbecue.

MARIE. Did I?

ROBERT. Where's the black one with a pattern?

MARIE. How do you remember what I wore to the barbecue?

ROBERT. You spilt something on it. I had to get it dry-cleaned. You looked pretty in it. Who knows what I remember...? I seem to be remembering Mary... what was her name? Goose fat. I really think her name was Mary. I remember it being similar to your name.

MARIE. I'll take that as a compliment.

ROBERT. Take it as you like for who you like for what you like.

The phone begins to ring.

MARIE *looks at* ROBERT.

It's too early yet...

MARIE *exits.*

ROBERT *coughs and then coughs.*

He touches his chest. He allows himself a look of pain.

He picks up the photographs again. He looks through them.

He laughs.

Now there's a profit.

Barely two strips of material.

Still, if it works for her.

It certainly… Marie? Marie… Oh.

He'd forgotten she was on the phone.

He looks at the pad and the pen.

He takes off his glasses. He puts them on the bedside cabinet.

He swings his legs over the side of the bed, breathes and then stands up.

He takes a breath, wobbles slightly, and sits back on the bed.

He looks around.

He stands again. Walks determinedly forward, wobbles.

Fuck.

And then crumples. To the ground.

Fuck.

He attempts to stop his fall, he attempts to move back towards the bed. He accomplishes neither. He lands harder than feels right. He coughs and then coughs again.

Fuck.

He laughs.

(*Faux voice.*) 'Nine cabinet members will fall.'

He laughs again.

Stupid fucking pricks.

He coughs and then coughs repeatedly.

He holds his hand over his mouth.

He looks at his hand and then smears it over his pyjamas.

The bloodstain stays where it is.

He looks around the room.

He pulls himself over to the wall.

He tries to get traction.

He tries to pull himself up.

He fails.

MARIE *comes in the room.*

She looks at him.

She looks at him a long, long time; he smiles at her.

MARIE. Bit of a…

ROBERT. The problem came when I decided to dance.

MARIE *laughs.*

Then looks at him a bit longer.

MARIE. Do you want…?

ROBERT. No.

MARIE. That was Hannah. She wanted to wish you good luck.

ROBERT. Did she?

MARIE. I told her you didn't need luck. You were a Tony target seat.

ROBERT. Twenty-two. I'm twenty-two. Target seat twenty-two.

MARIE. You don't need luck, you need Armageddon.

ROBERT. Am I – covered up…?

MARIE. You've a bloodstain on your left thigh.

ROBERT. Little John. I can't see if Little John is showing his head.

MARIE. No… No.

She smiles.

No. I don't know why it would matter to you. But no… Nor Robin Hood.

ROBERT. I always – Brighton bomb – and my abiding memory – was Norman on the television being dragged from the rubble – in his pyjamas – a man that really shouldn't have survived, and he was trying –

He starts laughing.

– this great moment – this greatest – defiant –'Listen to me,
IRA, you will not disturb our Government, our Norman
Tebbit can survive everything you throw at him' – and then
you realised, then you realised, everyone realised watching
him – the news cameras watching him – that he was desperately – trying desperately to cover his testicles up because his
pyjama trousers had been ripped by the blast.

MARIE *is not laughing.*

MARIE *thinks and then moves towards him, but she doesn't
help him up, instead she slowly gets on the floor.*

She lies down beside him.

They say nothing.

Will you light me a cigarette?

MARIE *thinks, and then sits up and takes a packet of ciga-
rettes from the bedside drawer – she doesn't stand up, just
leans across for them, lights the cigarette, takes a few puffs,
and then puts it into* ROBERT*'s mouth. She stays sitting up.
He stays lying down.*

I was thinking – this evening – for my – speech –

MARIE. Your – you finished…?

ROBERT….nothing – too – Secret is, not to get on TV when you
lose as – someone told me – may have been Willie – no, I was
thinking what I considered my greatest achievements. I was
making – a list. In my head.

She leans against the door.

MARIE. In your head?

ROBERT. It wasn't a long list.

MARIE. You haven't started it yet, have you?

*He looks at her, irritated. She smiles, trying to swallow her
irritation. And rubs her arm.*

ROBERT. It wasn't a… And the events seemed so – I resolved
the pensions problem when British Gas privatised.

MARIE. You were always great at the detail of things…

ROBERT. I did some important work restructuring the prisons subsection of the Home Office. Work people were grateful for – but significant – I was always good at the detail of things…

MARIE. Great at the detail of things…

ROBERT. Pennies. Pounds. Never headlines.

MARIE. Who needs headlines?

Pause. ROBERT takes the cigarette from his mouth and hands it to MARIE, who smokes some of it.

ROBERT. Do you know a man I always admired – Roy Jenkins…

MARIE. Roy Jenkins? That's a leap.

ROBERT. Not – I didn't agree with anything he did –

MARIE. Roy… Jenkins?

ROBERT. Didn't concern himself with the ladder. If they didn't like him, he'd dazzle them…

MARIE. He was just as ambitious as the rest of you. More so.

ROBERT. And the things he got done. As Home Secretary: legalisation of abortion, legalisation of homosexuality, abolition of the death penalty –

MARIE. Sounds like a shopping list for Sodom and Gomorrah –

ROBERT. No one wanted, Wilson was a… But he worked at it – abortion – back-door work – excuse the –

MARIE puts the cigarette back into ROBERT's mouth.

MARIE. Abortions. Sodom and Gomorrah –

ROBERT. He looked down the private members' bill list – told them he'd make sure they'd have time on the floor if they supported one of his measures. Hey presto. He hooked David Steel. Steel got all the credit, but it was Roy…

MARIE. I don't think there's any credit involved.

ROBERT *is flushing again.*

ROBERT. Then Europe. The Labour Party then hated the idea of – far more angry about it than we are now… Roy got the 'Yes' vote, Roy got us in.

MARIE. Ted was the one who… Not that there's any –

ROBERT. Without Roy he'd have never succeeded. That hung on a knife edge, it was Roy… Never Prime Minister, but the changes he made… The changes he made…

MARIE. He was Home Secretary. He was Chancellor. You did your job.

ROBERT. He did great things. He – found – mountains to move. And I think what I – did – didn't –

MARIE. Calm – slow down –

ROBERT. He changed lives – here – there – fucking everywhere –

MARIE. I don't like it when you swear –

ROBERT. And I sorted out the pensions black hole in a –

MARIE. Robert. Please.

ROBERT (*fully full*). I did nothing. I look back on – I should have been. I wasn't, and I should have been a – great man. I always thought I'd be a great man, and I wasn't. I just – wasn't.

Beat.

He makes a yelping noise.

Beat.

He makes half a yelping noise.

Beat. MARIE *doesn't look at him. Then she does. Then she doesn't again.*

MARIE. David Steel bought me a white wine spritzer once. I was wearing the red dress with the legs. I tried to decline it, but he was very persistent. You were talking to – someone –

or waiting to – he seemed less inclined to talk to anyone. He kept telling me it was only half wine, so it didn't count.

Roy was a nasty piece of lechery too. Sodom and Gomorrah. He'd have fitted in. Party hands.

Beat. MARIE *pulls a pillow down from the bed and puts it behind* ROBERT.

She then reaches further for a pillow for her. She puts it behind her head.

MARIE. Do you remember the first seat we tried for...?

ROBERT. Winchester.

MARIE. And for some reason – I was sitting at the back – for some reason you spent the entire meeting looking at me.

ROBERT. That probably was a mistake.

MARIE. Staring at me and only me. You were nervous.

ROBERT. I was petrified. I vomited three times in the toilets at Reading Station.

MARIE. And I reassured you. Looking at me reassured you.

ROBERT. It always did.

MARIE. And that was – the most wonderful – the most wonderful thing... For me. But I felt this great pressure, that my nerves not show, that I was there for you, and that I had to – absorb you to be – useful. Nerves must not show. I – absorbed – for you.

Pause. She pulls herself up to sitting.

Maybe I should write your speech. Tell the Liberal Democrats that yellow washes them out and that Labour one that I think she has issues she needs to talk about with her mother. Or her father. Or possibly both.

He touches her arm. She looks at the arm. And then at the bloodstain.

It's going to take bleach to get that out.

ROBERT. Yes.

She looks at his face, carefully, as if remembering it.

MARIE. When we got here – we won – and we fitted. And, uh…

ROBERT. Yes?

Pause. She picks up his hand, and plays with the webbing between his fingers.

MARIE. When Hannah – Hannah was – when Hannah was born you were debating a bill on out-of-town shopping centres –

ROBERT. That? It was a three-line whip and they'd suspended – the – thing – system.

MARIE. But I had my mother with me. So that was – fine.

ROBERT. I phoned as soon as I could…

MARIE. I let you listen to her breathe.

ROBERT. And then I had – to get off the line. There was a – I needed to be back in the chamber –

Pause.

MARIE. And you told me – you told me 'well done'. You said: 'I have to go now, Marie, but well done.'

Then Hannah had a few troubles settling down at night and you told me that we weren't to have any more kids, because your schedule didn't allow for it, and I let you do that. Then we sent her to St Mary's at an age where I didn't think she was ready, but you thought it'd be good for her as it was a – great – school… I wanted to go back to work, and you said that – I couldn't. You said I should come and be a secretarial support – well, I tried that, but I didn't like how you treated me. Like a secretary-wife, not a wife any more, not a – wife. So most days – most days I took to either filling with a letter to Hannah or the radio or filling with – groups and… And I'm not much of a joiner-in. So eventually I just – waited for you.

I did my keep-fit when that started on breakfast television, but mostly I waited for you to come home. I always just –

because you, because we – ever since you were that young man with the strange smile who couldn't talk to me in church. Ever since then.

Beat. She's remembering things now.

When Hannah got sick –

ROBERT. Marie –

MARIE. The first night in hospital – so pale and thin and – yellow. So yellow. I worried in case she breathed in too fiercely and her ribs cracked. And even she – even she –

Suddenly, her voice gets louder, goes from soft to loud in two paces.

Tweedledum or Tweedledee phoned me once – by accident – they were wanting… you. But they said, they kept me on the line, they didn't need to keep me on the line, but they clearly felt they needed to keep talking – why they thought they had to talk to – Conservative Central Office keeping MPs' wives entertained. They told me – this must have been twelve months ago – longer – Hestletine was doing something with someone and it had them concerned and they said – they said what an important person you were to them, and that to be sure to pass on that your support for John will have ramifications for… They started talking about the Hestletine ancestry and how we'd understand what it was to be humble Tories not related to Charles Dibdin and then they started explaining who Charles Dibdin was… And I said I knew who Charles Dibdin…

She turns and looks at him and then looks away. She spits the word out.

Humble. Humble.

You don't think I'm angry? I'm furious! To be thrown away like a used tissue, and not for reason of what you did, by voters who you served. Because it's time for change and 'that's politics'. You're not John Major, you never ran the Party, you never got close. Back to basics. Sleaze. You were basic. You were good. You were a good local MP, and you've always done a good job and now you're – not. And that's not fair. That's not how jobs are decided. That's not how I thought this would end.

But I will not have you feel a failure. That's not – you – I was very proud – of you. I didn't always agree with what you said, what you made me do, but I was you. I was you. We were you. I was you at the fêtes, and the visits, and the dinners, I was always proud to be you. And that's – that's – and I'm – that's that.

There is a long pause.

She can't look at him and he can't look at her.

Then the phone starts ringing.

They listen to it.

It rings for an age.

Then eventually rings off.

Who do you think?

ROBERT. Probably them. The results are getting close. They want us down at the count.

MARIE. Do you think?

ROBERT. It's about the right time.

MARIE. We'll use your chair.

ROBERT. Yes. Chair doesn't matter now.

MARIE *stands up.*

It takes her a moment, she catches her breath.

He looks at her strong back.

Do I need – to apologise?

Beat.

MARIE. No. No. You never did listen properly. No.

Beat. She doesn't turn around, she sets herself and then she does turn.

Come on, if you get up quick, I'll let you look at the girl in a bikini again before we have to get going...

She slowly, gently, helps him up.

Slowly. Slowly.

He stops halfway and takes a breath, and then, just like that, he's standing again and it's almost beautiful; she puts her hands on his waist.

There.

ROBERT. Yes. There.

MARIE. Okay?

ROBERT. Yes. Okay.

MARIE. Okay?

ROBERT. Yes. Yes.

MARIE. Okay.

Pause. He sways slightly.

ROBERT. What am I going to do?

MARIE. When?

ROBERT. Now. What am I going to – do?

MARIE. You'll do all sorts. We'll do all sorts. We'll take walks in the park, we'll buy a new cookery book and experiment with different things for dinner each night, we'll take drives down to see Hannah and take her food and check she's okay, we'll find friends to play cards with, we'll go to every constituency Party meeting, every branch meeting, we'll find programmes we want to watch together on television, we'll garden and win a rosette in the 'Town in Bloom' competition, we'll enjoy ourselves, we'll settle.

ROBERT. Settle?

MARIE. It's what old people do.

They look at each other. Then she leans in and softly kisses his lips.

ROBERT. I'm suddenly quite hungry.

MARIE. Are you?

ROBERT. Shall we get some chips? On the way to the results…

She softly smiles at him.

MARIE. If you'd like.

ROBERT. Dr Phillips wouldn't like it.

MARIE. No. He would not.

ROBERT. But I don't like Dr Phillips.

MARIE. He's a funny way about him, doesn't he?

ROBERT. He told me last time – he said: (*Nasal voice.*) 'In the interests of transparency, I should tell you, sir, I'm intending on voting Blair.'

MARIE. Right.

ROBERT. 'In the interests of transparency…'

MARIE *laughs.*

MARIE. 'In the interests of transparency…'

ROBERT. 'In the interests of transparency.'

She thinks, and then gently kisses him again, on the cheek and then the lips.

She pulls back and looks at him.

MARIE. Have you written anything? Have you anything to say?

He smiles, and shakes his head with a twinkle.

ROBERT. Maybe it doesn't matter. Maybe I'll write something in the car. Maybe – I'll sing.

Pause. She smiles.

MARIE. You were my great man.

ROBERT. Was I?

MARIE. Yes. You were.

    ROBERT *thinks*.

ROBERT. Yes. Let's get chips.

    Slow fade to black.

    End of Part One.

PART TWO

2.41 a.m.

A tidy bedsit. SARAH *enters first, she's drunk, but not especially so you'd notice immediately.* IAN *isn't drunk.*

SARAH. Oh, it's not that messy…

IAN. It's not tidy.

SARAH. With the bed to the side…

IAN. And the sofa… there… you want to sit down?

SARAH. I want to look around.

IAN. Looking for what?

SARAH. I just want to poke…

I like people poking about my house.

I like people being intrigued.

IAN *smiles.*

IAN. Then we should have gone to yours… I could have been intrigued at [yours] –

SARAH. No, I followed you… If you had followed me we could have gone back to mine.

But I made the move, so I won a trip to your house.

She starts to poke about. IAN *looks at his hands.*

My mum used to love poking about my room – poke – poke – one time she found an old toothbrush she insisted I was using as a dildo. I was fifteen years old – she said, 'Lots of girls have very healthy sexual appetites at your age, I know I did, but it's a very confusing as well as perfectly natural time.'

IAN *laughs.* SARAH *looks at him.*

IAN. My dad just gave me a book. *Your Body and You*.

SARAH. 'It's perfectly natural, do you want to talk about it? The dildo?' No, she called it something else. She called it something – I can't remember – I think she may have called it a 'sexual device'. Truth was, she'd heard about it on Radio 4 – *Woman's Hour* did dildos. Sexual devices.

But the truth also was that I had a new pair of Doc Martens and I was proud of them and mud and shit kept getting caught in the tread, because it was quite deep tread, so I used a toothbrush to… True story. Bet I don't look like a woman who used to wear Docs as a kid.

Maybe I do. Do I?

IAN. You could…

SARAH. You should have seen the toothbrush – I mean, you must wonder what she thought I had up my fanny. The toothbrush was… not clean. It was brown. The bristles were brown. I mean, really quite… really quite… not nice.

IAN *isn't sure how to respond, so just smiles.*

Pause. She continues to try and behave casually as she pokes through his stuff. Eventually, she needs to break the silence…

What shall I do with my coat?

IAN. Oh. Just put it anywhere.

SARAH. I hate phrases like that. 'Just put it anywhere.' I feel like shouting at the screen – 'It's your dick, put it in her fanny.'

She starts to take off her shoes, they look like they've hurt her feet.

IAN. Do you?

SARAH. Sorry, am I being confrontational? It's a mixture of drunkenness and fear of sex.

IAN. Right.

She gives her shoes to IAN. *Who doesn't quite know what to do with them, and so puts them down beside himself. In the centre of the room. It's an odd place for shoes. She looks at where he's put them. She looks at him. Slightly accusingly.*

SARAH. Don't worry. I'm not going to take the rest of my clothes off and hand them to you…

IAN. Not that – no.

She laughs. He doesn't know why.

SARAH. You were giving as good as you got at the party…

IAN. No. I wasn't –

SARAH. You fucking were, wideboy.

IAN. No. Was I?

SARAH. What was it you said… I can't remember how you said it… You said something about Blair being one bollock short of a mouthful.

IAN. I didn't.

SARAH. 'The thing about Tony Blair is, he's one bollock short of a mouthful.'

IAN. I think you've got me mixed up.

SARAH. 'One bollock short of a mouthful.' It's a lovely phrase. I was quite surprised at a Liberal Democrat…

IAN. I think… that was probably James.

SARAH. James?

IAN. James. Yes. James. He came with me. Wiry hair. Grey jacket.

I'm not much of a talker. You were mostly talking to him.

I was there. But you two talked.

He's not really a Liberal Democrat.

Beat. SARAH *appraises the situation.*

SARAH. And what happened to James?

IAN. Um. Well…

He, uh… He had to go home.

SARAH *bullet laughs and then bullet laughs again*.

SARAH. I went home with the wrong guy.

IAN. No.

SARAH (*really laughing*). I went home with the wrong guy.

IAN. It's – um – Did you?

SARAH. Jesus. Am I that drunk?

Pause.

James.

IAN. We work together. He's a good friend. Well. Colleague.

Wiry hair. Grey jacket. Do you want to leave?

SARAH. Fuck no. This is exciting. This is like 'Guess Who?'
but… sexual. 'Sexual Guess Who?' Awesome.

She's staring at him quite intently.

IAN. Do you want the TV on? We could check what's –

SARAH. See how far you've lost yet…

IAN. Well. Not really about the winning.

Not that it's about the taking part either…

SARAH *laughs again*.

SARAH. It *was* a good party. 'Sexual Guess Who?' Who are
you?

IAN. Who am I?

SARAH (*Cilla Black impression*). 'Hello number two, what's
your name and where do you come from?'

IAN. Don't…

She laughs again. He doesn't know why. Again.

SARAH. The Party party?

IAN. What?

SARAH. A Party having a party – funny when you – I thought that was funny – a Party having a party – Who was I talking about that with…? Did we talk at all?

IAN. Of course we did… we, um… we talked about the Millennium Bug.

SARAH. I only went because my friend Ruth told me free – booze… 'Come to the Party party.' It might have been her I was – talking about it with.

IAN. Yeah? Yeah. That's sort of why James came… We don't really… It's open-door. We talked about restricting, but…

SARAH. I can fit my whole fist in my mouth. Can you do that?

IAN. What? Can you?

SARAH. Sorry – party – party tricks, that's the way my brain works, I won't show you. It's painful and makes me look very unattractive.

IAN. I'm sure it doesn't.

SARAH. Well… it does…

Pause.

IAN. There was a guy at my school whose party trick was he could fit his whole penis in an eggcup.

Pause. SARAH *barks a laugh and then stops.*

SARAH. Jesus.

IAN. What?

SARAH. 'Hello, Cilla, my name is…'

IAN. Ian. We definitely did the names thing… You're Sarah.

SARAH. 'And I am a… Liberal Democrat, Cilla.'

IAN. Housing Officer. I'm a Housing Officer.

Pause. SARAH *tries to think of a response to that. She fails. She barks another laugh.*

SARAH. Have you got any alcohol?

IAN. Good idea. What would you like?

SARAH. I would like a pint of water and a large glass of red wine…

IAN. That… I can do…

SARAH. Good.

> IAN *exits.* SARAH *looks around his room. She picks a book out. Will Hutton* – The State We're In. *She flicks through. She smiles. She reads a page. She calls off…*

You write notes in the margins of your books.

> IAN *reappears. Suddenly. Anxiously.*

IAN. Not really.

SARAH. You've written an exclamation mark beside a – you've written an exclamation mark – what does it say?

IAN. Don't read it out.

> SARAH *reads the paragraph. She reads it again. She frowns. She puts the book back on the shelf.*

SARAH. Do you do it for your fiction books too? Do you underline your fiction books? Or is it only facts – are you only interested in facts or do you underline a choice phrase or two in fiction? A lovely Dickens – sentence or a Shakespearean thing. Do you underline?

IAN. Um. Some. Sometimes.

SARAH. What about letters? Do you underline letters?

IAN. Who from?

SARAH. The bank. British Gas. Friends. Family. Lovers. Letters from other people. So you can skim-read them and not have to…

IAN. No. Not… Well. Some[times] –

SARAH. Yeah? Interesting.

IAN. Um… yeah, just… when things matter – I like to remember them.

SARAH shifts her weight from one foot to the other. She looks at IAN. For some reason she likes this.

SARAH. Do you?

IAN. Yeah.

SARAH. Yeah.

IAN thinks, and then exits again. SARAH looks around, sees the bed and stalks over to it. She looks at it a moment and then suddenly pulls back the duvet. She laughs at herself. She touches the sheets underneath. And then bends and smells the sheets. Then she laughs. Then she calls out.

You don't mind if I check your sheets, do you?

IAN re-enters on the bounce.

IAN. What?

He looks at the bed.

SARAH. I slept with one guy – the other day, I am a bit of a slut, by the way – whose sheets were so greasy, it almost made me sick. They smelt of old sweat and greasy hair and they were horrible to sleep on. Horrible.

I'm not promising anything, just better to know the full facts before making a decision. As the bishop said to the abortionist.

With his thumb up her bottom… Or…

He thinks of how to respond to that, he can't, he exits. He re-enters, carrying a tray of drinks, he puts them down on his coffee table. He smoothes down a cushion and puts it where she might sit on the sofa. Then he sits on the other sofa. He doesn't look at her the entire time. He can't. This whole thing is slightly too real.

IAN. Why don't we…? We could drink these sitting down… Watch the…

He puts on the TV. He looks at what's happening.

She watches him with a smile. He turns and looks at her. He calculates what he's just done.

Sorry.

SARAH. No.

IAN. That was…

He turns off the TV miserably.

SARAH. Not for me. Don't turn off for me. You can have the… It's your party.

They sit in silence. Then he thinks and turns on some music. He's not sure what's in his hi-fi. It's Donna Summer. He turns and looks at her.

IAN. Sorry.

She looks at him for a long time. She's trying to work him out.

SARAH. For which bit?

IAN. Which bit?

SARAH. Do you change them before every Party party – in case you get lucky? Or do you save the bed for best and normally sleep on the floor wrapped in a towel?

IAN. What?

SARAH. The sheets. They're clean, Mr Sheen.

IAN. Oh.Yes. Truth is, my mum's coming round tomorrow – so I cleaned.

SARAH. So this *is* clean, and you were being a little camp about 'It's so messy'. What time's she getting here?

IAN. Oh, don't worry, not 'til lunchtime…

SARAH. So when I do stay over, you mean, I will have ample time to escape before I humiliate you?

IAN. No, no, I didn't mean… I just meant you probably had work. I mean, if you stay. It's when, not… if… I mean… I don't know what I'm saying.

She's looking at him closely now. She smiles.

SARAH. No, okay.

IAN. Sorry. Pathetic is as pathetic does, and…

She smiles. And holds eye contact.

SARAH. Are you pathetic? Number two. Ian.

Oh God, I am drunk, I'm feeling quite emotional. I need to pee.

Other people cry when they get emotional, I just need to pee. Same waterworks, different button, as my mum always used to – no. I can hold it.

Pause. She stands up, downs the pint of water in one easy chug, and starts dancing. In fact, she does a little dance for him. She wants him to join in, but doesn't indicate he should. When he doesn't join in, the dance becomes a little elongated, in a sort of odd way. It lasts for about forty seconds. Then SARAH stands there looking shy.

I don't normally get this drunk.

IAN. Okay.

SARAH. I mean, I'm a slut, granted. But I normally go home with the guy I fancied, not the other guy.

IAN starts to gently laugh. SARAH laughs too.

SARAH. I like that. You're humourful.

IAN. Sorry. I'm just… I don't do this much and this is becoming increasingly – surreal. If you want to leave…

SARAH. 'Surreal'?

Pause. She doesn't leave. Neither say anything for a long time. She does some more hip-swayage/dancing. He looks at his hands. IAN is not good at silence.

IAN. I just – don't know what you're doing here…

Pause.

Did you vote?

SARAH. Are you nice, Ian?

IAN. I'd like to be.

SARAH. How nice?

IAN. Uh, in, um – in what respect?

SARAH. If I was to ask a hundred of your friends – in a very *Family Fortunes*-type way – I was Cilla Black, I am Les Dennis – I am Les Dennis in a very Jeremy-Beadle-type disguise – even given myself tits – I am Les Dennis and we asked a hundred of your friends: 'What do you think of when you think of Ian?' – And your friends – would they say: 'He's nice'?

IAN *considers this and smiles.*

IAN. Yeah. They probably would. Which probably makes me extraordinarily dull.

SARAH. Not really.

People say they hate the word 'nice' because it's meaningless. I actually think it's got a very specific meaning.

It's about a glow, isn't it? Or a –

IAN. Maybe.

Pause. She looks at him even more carefully. He's feeling slightly intimidated.

SARAH. Yes. It's a glow. A glow. A glow in the dark. A Glow-in-the-Dark Batman. Did you have a Glow-in-the-Dark Batman when you were a kid?

IAN. No.

SARAH stops for a moment, flexes her arm, shifts her weight, and then turns and looks at him again.

She makes a Family Fortunes *buzzer noise. 'Bi-baa.' She laughs. He sort of laughs. She looks at him, her face has sunk slightly.*

SARAH. Will you be nice to me if I told you some stuff?

IAN. I'm a good listener, if that's what you –

SARAH (*she sings*).
> Cross over the road, my friend,
> Ask the Lord His strength to lend,
> His compassion has no end,
> Cross over the road.

IAN. Stop.

SARAH. Did you have to sing that in school?

IAN. Sarah…

SARAH. I feel like an eleven-year-old girl…

IAN. Sarah…

SARAH. Then again, I feel like an eleven-year-old most of the time.

She approaches, she indicates what she wants, they kiss slowly. He breaks off.

He looks at her a long, long time.

IAN. I think you…

She kisses him again. They break off. She licks her lips. She takes off her top. It's a bit of a struggle, being drunk her arms don't fit through the holes and her head is a struggle and a half.

No… No.

SARAH. Take off your top.

She undoes her bra. He looks at her tits. They scare him. They're not scary tits. But for him…

IAN. I thought you wanted to, uh, talk about something.

SARAH. Enough talking –

She kisses him again. She pulls up his top. He resists, she pulls it off quite aggressively. She slides her hand down his body.

Nipples. I have nipples. Do you like my nipples? I think they look like raspberries two days past their best…

IAN. That's…

36

SARAH. You wouldn't be taking advantage… Think of it like a
punctuation mark. A full stop. Or maybe a semi-colon.

*She opens his fly, and puts her hand inside. He tries to stop
her. She giggles.*

Take it back. A colon.

He pulls his hips back from her.

IAN. Sarah… Stop. Let's talk –

SARAH (*all fire*). NO! You weren't interested in talking.

IAN dislocates. Both are surprised by her outburst.

Sorry. Didn't mean to shout.

She makes the Family Fortunes *buzzer noise again.*

Wrong, Sarah. Wrong.

She kisses him again. This time she misses his mouth.

If you're worried you'll be raping me. I consent.

She picks up his phone. She speaks into it.

I consent.

She puts the phone down.

IAN. Please. I think we should stop.

She does stop. She looks at him.

SARAH. 'We'? No 'we' in it, really, was there?

She wobbles.

Are you a Christian? Most Liberal Democrats I meet are
Christians. Not that I meet many Liberal Democrats.

She sways slightly.

IAN. I think you should go home. I don't think you want this –

*He looks at her slowly. He picks up his top and starts to put it
back on. She stops him with an easy hand. They stand there,
semi-naked, in the middle of his room. She seemingly doesn't
notice. But she looks oddly vulnerable nonetheless.*

SARAH. When I was younger I knew a boy called Ian – and, uh… he was the love of my life. A nice boy, odd like you, he used to walk in front of me when we walked in the park. Why? So he could kill any snakes hiding in the grass.

IAN. I don't take – advantage – of people.

SARAH. He was eleven, so it wasn't an affectation. So it's nothing to be admired…

IAN. It's not about being good – just… it wouldn't be that – fun –

SARAH. And then we met up when he was older and we had sex a few times and actually he was really odd.

He'd only have sex with me in the bath. It was fine, felt a bit sticky at the end but, uh, not too bad.

She turns on Donna Summer again, and turns it right up.

Strangest rim. Got the strangest rim around it. The bath. All sorts of liquids float to the top when you have sex in the bath. Had to scrub it with Clorox. One time – one time he persuaded me to have sex in the bath when I was on my period. Like *Jaws*! Now that was a rim! Doesn't matter. Anyway.

IAN. What's –

SARAH leans in and whispers in his ear. She continues to do so for up to a minute. The thing she tells him devastates him.

SARAH. And now we've talked. And now you've listened.

She laughs. Then does a half-hearted attempt at the Family Fortunes *buzzer noise.*

He just stands there.

IAN. On the street –

SARAH. No.

IAN. On the street –

SARAH. No, no. I don't want to talk about it…

IAN. But –

SARAH. No. No. You said you were a good listener. Not a good talker. I don't need a talker.

They sit in silence for a moment, she turns her hand over and looks at it carefully. She looks at her tits. She thinks about covering up her nudity, but changes her mind.

She notices a mark on her skirt and scratches at it.

He tries not to look at her. Then he does look at her, very deliberately.

IAN *gently takes her hand. She looks at his hand. Then she disentangles herself from it, reaches out and takes a glass of wine and slurps.*

SARAH. What is this fucking music?

IAN. Donna Summer.

SARAH. Right.

IAN walks across and turns it off.

She takes another slurp on her wine.

SARAH. I just wanted to tell someone – needed to – someone who wasn't – who didn't want to make me a fucking cup of tea and put their fingers on my forehead – I've done so much of that – I told you because you're not a talker, but you seem nice. And you have a very nice bum. And you didn't want to take advantage of me.

IAN. But –

SARAH. Now – (*She puts her hands over his eyes.*) say one about me, one feature about me, and it can't be bum, because I said that, or eyes, mouth, or legs because they're boring.

Or personality.

Definitely not personality.

Or cunt or tits, because –

Or belly button.

I had an ex-boyfriend who said belly button. I liked that as an answer, but then he kept licking it during sex, which is not what I meant at all… And it's put me off belly-button people for life, so don't be one of them.

IAN. You've got nice ears…

SARAH. Okay. Go on…

SARAH takes a moment to herself to show the full anguish of what's happened to her. This isn't big, it's small and controlled, but it's immensely private and the hand over IAN's eyes means it's kept that way.

IAN. What?

SARAH. You have to describe them. You can't have just thought it up. So describe them – just to prove you weren't lying…

IAN. I don't…

SARAH. Big? Small? Do they stick out? To what degree do they stick out?

Pause.

IAN. You're – very brave.

She releases his eyes and kisses him aggressively. He breaks off. She sighs.

You are. You're very – brave.

She looks at him.

SARAH. No, I'm not.

She was my life and now she's not and that's – that's not bravery. That's tragedy.

IAN. My mum's dying, she's – um – she's coming up tomorrow to go see a cancer – I mean, it's just boring cancer.

SARAH. Okay –

IAN. I wasn't saying – it's not the same.

SARAH. No, it's not.

Pause.

IAN. When she told me. My dad left her – I'm sort of the most important person in her life. I wasn't quite sure what to say or do. I wanted to laugh. I'm better at it now, she's coming up to see a specialist. I arranged it.

SARAH. Good for you.

IAN. Did you ever – when my granddad died – I remember going with my dad to the funeral – and we had to sing a hymn. 'We Plough the Fields and Scatter.' Or something like –

SARAH *smiles*.

SARAH. I know it. It's no 'Cross Over the Road'. But it's a hymn.

IAN. Did you know it has two possible tunes that can go with it? My grandma chose it because of one of these tunes, but you don't specify a tune to go with the hymn when choosing hymns and the organist chose to play the other tune. Which no one can sing along with. So this – small crematorium – that I was in – stood there and tried desperately to mumble their way through this hymn that they didn't know... Mostly old people, mumbling their – all consonants and – I started to laugh.

SARAH. It sounds funny.

IAN. But I was standing by my dad – who'd lost his dad – and he was about to give the speech – whatever you call those speeches and I shouldn't have laughed.

Pause.

I'm not very good with death.

SARAH. Is anyone?

IAN. Yeah. Some people are.

Pause.

I'm not very good at many things, really...

SARAH. No.

IAN. I feel like I should – I mean...

41

She stands and walks towards him.

Shouldn't we… talk… Talking with my mum was…

She stops when she's standing in front of him.

SARAH. Do you want to know the best thing about whispering?

IAN. No.

SARAH. If you do it quiet enough you can't hear what you're saying…

SARAH *laughs*.

SARAH. Today's the birthday. Anniversary. May first. Mayday. Of the… I wasn't with a friend. Many wanted to be with me. My ex-husband wanted to be with me. But I was walking around the streets, and then I saw this party with the lights on and – you all looked very happy. Why did you look so happy?

IAN. We're forecast to do well, tonight.

SARAH. You're forecast to do well, you looked happy. And so I went inside and here I am… With the wrong man in the wrong flat at the wrong time. But at least next year this'll be the anniversary of something else.

IAN. Yeah. The election or the…

IAN *nods*.

SARAH. Or you.

IAN. Or me.

They look at each other.

Pause. She picks up her top and pulls it on. She is finally not naked. This is a sort of good thing. It's also a full stop. IAN *semi-smiles.*

SARAH. Do you want to put the TV on?

Pause.

Go on. Put the telly on…

IAN *hesitates and then sits. And then he turns the telly on. She sits beside him.*

Have you won any yet?

IAN. Yeah.

She turns and looks at him with a gentle smile.

SARAH. But you're not going to win the whole thing? You can't win the whole thing?

IAN *laughs.*

IAN. Oh no… No… definitely not…

SARAH *laughs.*

SARAH. And who's that man?

IAN. That's, um, Portillo. Michael Portillo.

SARAH. Should I know him…?

IAN. No.

SARAH. He doesn't look happy.

IAN. No.

SARAH. Who's the other one?

IAN. I'm not sure.

SARAH. He looks happy.

IAN. Yeah.

Black.

End of Part Two.

PART THREE

7.37 a.m.

A teenage bedroom.

Two boys are sleeping with their arms around each other on a single teenage bed. WILL, eighteen, self-conscious, gently spooning JAKE, eighteen, conscious of self.

It's gentle. It's kind of beautiful.

JAKE wakes first, he realises where he is.

He realises whose arms are around him. He thinks.

He gently dislocates himself.

He sits up on the bed. He's wearing pyjamas. M&S crisp blue pyjamas, the sort of pyjamas that cost a bit.

He rubs his arms.

He exits the room.

WILL immediately opens his eyes. On the 'B' of the (gentle door) bang. As if he's been waiting for ages. He lies perfectly still. He adjusts his erection.

He smells his hand.

He looks scared.

He sits up.

He looks more scared.

He's wearing boxer shorts and a T-shirt. He stands and walks around the room, trying to conceal his erection. But it's hard because he's quite a big boy.

He opens a drawer, he looks inside. He picks out a pair of socks. He examines them.

He hears a noise.

He lies down again.

He then shuts his eyes as JAKE *re-enters the room.*

JAKE *has a stack of newspapers. All the tabloids. And an apple. Which is green. He sits cross-legged on the floor. He starts flicking through.*

He stops at a page. He covers it over. He talks in a whisper.

JAKE. Jack Cunningham –

Jack Cunningham –

Jack Cunningham –

Jack Cunningham –

JAKE *stands and begins to strip out of his pyjamas.*

He stops and looks at WILL. *He carries on stripping.*

Jack Jack Jack Jack. Jack in the box.

He picks out a pair of briefs from his chest of drawers.

He puts them on. Delicately, and with a little sorrow as if he enjoyed the nudity.

Then he takes a shirt out of his wardrobe and puts that on.

JAKE. Cunningham Cunningham –

Richie Cunningham Richie Cunningham –

Jack in the box. Cunningham –

Richie Cunningham in a box. Richie Cunningham in a box. Richie Cunningham in a box. *Happy Days* are dead. Jack Cunningham.

He sits in his pants and shirt and looks at the page.

WILL *opens his eyes and looks at* JAKE.

JAKE *covers the page over.*

WILL *closes his eyes again.*

Alistair Darling Alistair Darling –

Alistair Alistair Alistair –

He does up his shirt buttons and finds a pair of black trousers, he pulls them on.

Then starts putting on his school tie.

He looks at WILL *again.*

He raises his voice slightly.

Darling Darling Darling –

Will you check the stairs, Darling?

I love you, Darling, will you check the stairs?

I love your stairs, Darling.

Darling Darling Darling, Will, are you awake?

WILL *says nothing.*

Will… because you're not making any noise at all, and normally, when people sleep,they make some noise, so are you awake?

Beat.

WILL *opens his eyes, thinks, and then closes them again.*

And then opens them.

WILL. Uh. Yeah.

JAKE. Did I… [wake you]?

WILL. No.

JAKE. How long have you been…?

WILL. I don't…

JAKE. Yeah?

WILL. How long since I made a noise? I mean, it's probably… I should make more… I'll remember that for next time…

JAKE. Yeah.

Beat.

Yeah.

WILL. What are you...?

JAKE. Remembering the cabinet. Memorising. Trying to. I figured Sharpey might... Sorry, I'd have done it downstairs but Mum's asleep on the sofa again and Liz's in the kitchen trying to pretend like last night wasn't important and doing her nails really loudly. Which smelt. Nail polish. Which isn't even a good smell. Though, sort of sends you high, according to her.

WILL. Who've you got...?

JAKE. I'm starting with the... You heard about Frank Dobson?

WILL. No.

JAKE. Straight in. Health Secretary. They think.

WILL. Yeah?

JAKE. Yeah.

WILL. Wow.

JAKE. Yeah. Pretty huge.

WILL. I don't even know... where he came from...

JAKE. Select committees, I think. I mean, no... I don't know. It's a big promotion...

He looks for and reads.

Environment. He was environment. Shit. I should have... [known] that. Which is now – I think, Prescott. Part of Prescott's super ministry, have you? Oh. That's...

JAKE*'s radio alarm suddenly goes off.*

It's 'Things Can Only Get Better' by D:Ream.

JAKE *smiles at* WILL, *does a little dance,* WILL *sort of copies him. They do a strange unrehearsed semi-synchronised dance.*

JAKE *starts miming the singing. Then turns it off. Halfway through a sentence.*

WILL. Wow.

JAKE. Yeah. Yeah.

Beat. WILL *thinks and then sits up.*

WILL. Did we – drink a lot last night?

JAKE. No. Not…

WILL. We didn't.

JAKE. No?

WILL. No.

JAKE. I mean, a bit… toasted a few in. Toasted a few out. Lots of toast. With red jam on top.

WILL *smiles.*

WILL. I thought we…

JAKE. A bit.

WILL. Yeah. Because we didn't top-and-tail and that… In bed, I mean…

JAKE. Yeah. Yeah. I wondered about that too.

WILL. Bladdered – probably –

JAKE. Yeah.

WILL. Frank Dobson.

JAKE. Yeah. For some reason I have no problem remembering his name. Frank Dobson. Dobbing in Frank's son. For some reason that's…

WILL *(laugh).* Dobbing in Frank – I'll remember…

JAKE. Dobbing in Frank's son. Yeah. Yeah. I'm all about the memory – aids –

WILL *counts visibly under his breath – one, two, three – and stands up. He looks down, his erection is no longer visible. He looks up,* JAKE *is looking at him strangely.*

WILL. What?

JAKE. And we played that card game.

WILL. Yeah? Do you think Sharpey will test us?

JAKE. Yeah. I don't know. Maybe… 'Be prepared', though, so… Dib-dib-dib.

WILL. Do you think I should…?

JAKE. I don't know.

Pause. JAKE smiles.

Oh, there's one you'll love – Dad bought me all the papers, left them on the doormat before he –

WILL. Wow. I like the way he…

JAKE. Yeah. He's cool.

He knew I'd want all the papers.

He's on a – he's quite cool with me at the moment because of the whole – you know – but he knew I'd want all the – and he's out of the house at five at the moment – so he must have went to the twenty-four-hour before…

WILL. Yeah. That's really cool.

JAKE. Anyway, one you'll like – the *Star*'s all – 'It's a new Dawn – um, actually her name is Gaynor.'

He searches through the stack and finds a copy of the Star. *It's got a picture of a topless model on the front (she's Gaynor).* WILL *laughs.*

WILL. Oh, that's really [funny] –

JAKE. Isn't it?

WILL. She's properly…

JAKE. I know.

WILL. Not really my [type] –

JAKE. No. Nor me. A bit…

WILL. Big.

JAKE. Yeah.

They both look at the picture again. Slightly scared.

Yeah. Big. Yeah. Well.

WILL. What did the *Guardian* say?

JAKE. Oh. He didn't buy that one, just the tabloids.

WILL. Right.

JAKE. I think he thought I'd just want the [tabloids], plus – they are a bit cheaper than the…

WILL. Yeah. Still. My dad would never…

JAKE. Your dad's great. I love talking to your dad.

WILL. Yeah. He's…

JAKE. No. Seriously. He's great. He's brilliant. He can fix things. My dad can literally fix nothing.

WILL. Yeah, that's – nothing's broken in my house.

JAKE. Well, nothing's broken in this house either. My dad just gets someone in.

WILL. Yeah.

JAKE laughs.

JAKE. I mean, who do you think irons my shirts? Mum?

WILL. Yeah.

JAKE. I mean… there's plenty that lady probably thinks she can do – but she can't – and even if she could – ironing shirts – not top of the list.

JAKE laughs. WILL looks at him.

WILL. Yeah.

JAKE gets some scissors and then sits on the floor and starts cutting out articles for his scrapbook.

JAKE. He left a note on the papers – 'Were you still up for Portillo?' Which I thought was quite –

WILL. Yeah.

JAKE. He probably heard it on the radio but still…

WILL. We were.

JAKE. Yeah.

WILL. We were still up for Rifkind, actually. Was that before or…?

JAKE. I can't remember.

WILL. We probably were still up when your dad got up to… I mean, we can't have got more than two hours… three hours…

JAKE. Yeah. I don't know when…

WILL. I don't feel tired.

JAKE. No?

WILL. No. Probably adrenalin. Or nail-polish fumes that have – transcended the [floors] –

JAKE. I bet Sharpey will make us do loads of stuff.

WILL. Maybe.

JAKE. I bet he'll…

WILL. Maybe. Still, I'm not tired so…

JAKE. No. I'm not saying I am. I'm not tired. I can always tell when I'm tired and hiding it from myself. I start to sing songs.

WILL. Great.

JAKE. And I'm not singing songs. Well, other than – do you think Carla will be in…?

WILL. Maybe.

JAKE. I bet she will. I'll bet she'll be done – all the – she'll know all the Cabinet off by…

WILL. Yeah. Probably. And then she'll give you that look she gives you when she gets stuff better than you.

JAKE. Yeah. Maybe.

WILL. Ever since you fingered her by the swings after the *Westminster Live* thing.

JAKE. Oh. Yeah.

WILL. Ever since you got into Cambridge and she [didn't] –

JAKE. Yeah. More that than…

WILL. Yeah.

JAKE. The finger. Ing. Though, I think if she'd applied for SPS rather than Law she'd have… definitely not got…

WILL. No. She's not as clever as you.

JAKE. She is. Carla. Definitely.

WILL. She isn't.

> JAKE *waves the scissors in the air.*

JAKE. She is. She got far better GCSEs…

WILL. What do they…? Anyway, you weren't even really trying then…

JAKE. Yeah.

WILL. She isn't.

JAKE. She is.

WILL. She isn't. It's what I like about you, you don't know how good you are. Clever. Good.

JAKE. Okay.

WILL. Not to…

JAKE. You've gone [red] –

WILL. No.

> JAKE *giggles, enjoying this.*

JAKE. Yeah, your cheeks are all… crimson. Silken crimson. Silken crimsssson.

WILL. Not really.

JAKE. I don't really fancy her any more anyway…

WILL. Carla?

JAKE. I mean, I never really did. I only – because she basically offered.

WILL. We were all quite drunk.

JAKE. Yeah. And then the fingering just sort of – I mean, she basically put my hand in her… knickers and – you know – I felt like – I mean, it was – I didn't even touch her tits, which was [odd]. Well, only through clothing. How does that – ? Twat touch but no nipple touch, that's a strange girl.

WILL. Yeah.

JAKE. Anyway, you got up to something that night, didn't you, with, uh…? With –

WILL. No.

JAKE. Not Tessa or Emma or someone…

WILL. No.

JAKE. I think Emma fancies you.

WILL. Does she?

JAKE. She told me the other day that you had really cute freckles.

WILL. Really cute [freckles]?

JAKE. Yeah. On your face.

WILL. Okay.

JAKE (*replicating Shaggy's 'Mr Boombastic'*). 'Mr Luvva Luvva.' She's not wrong…

WILL. What?

    JAKE *suddenly gets* WILL *in a headlock.*

    What? No. Get off.

    JAKE *sort of tries to do a sort of judo knuckle-crunch on the top of* WILL*'s head, and then he laughs and dislocates.*

JAKE. God.

WILL. Yeah.

> WILL *gingerly fingers his head.* JAKE *looks at him and laughs. And then smiles. And then frowns.*

JAKE. Emma.

WILL. Yeah.

JAKE. Emma.

WILL. Yeah.

JAKE. She's got a nice bum.

WILL. Has she?

JAKE. Yeah. And she's clever without being too clever. She's just the right sort of clever, I think. For a girlfriend.

WILL. Yeah?

JAKE. Yeah. Will you ask her out, then?

WILL. No. Not really my [type]. You could have fucked her. Carla. You could have…

JAKE. No…

WILL. You could.

JAKE. Not without build-up. And build-up's dull… Besides, I don't really have time at the moment anyway. For the dull build-up.

WILL. Yeah.

JAKE. Yeah. And twat not nipple is just…

> *Pause. The two boys look at each other. And then look away.*

Funny word… 'fucked'.

WILL. Yeah. I hate using it.

JAKE. So… big.

WILL. Yeah. Big.

JAKE. It's the 'F' – it's a brutal-sounding consonant. But sex sounds so…

WILL. Yeah. And making love! I mean!

JAKE. Shagging?

WILL. Bonking?

JAKE. Rutting?

WILL. Skootching.

JAKE. Mooching.

WILL. Banging.

JAKE. Donkey-Konging.

WILL. Hmmm-and-haaaing.

JAKE. Doing the do-se-do.

WILL. Meating – M-E-A-T-ing.

JAKE. Yeah.

WILL. Yeah.

JAKE. Yeah.

WILL. Shagging's probably better… best.

JAKE (*Churchill impression*). 'Democracy is the worst form of government apart from all the others…' You know. Churchill.

WILL (*laughs, sort of*). Yeah.

Beat.

JAKE. Aren't you going to get ready?

WILL. What?

JAKE. Changed. For school. I won't look.

WILL. Okay.

Pause. JAKE *thinks and then sets his chair from the desk so it's facing towards the audience. He sits in it. He faces front.*

He knows exactly what he's doing. He's got a prickish look in his eyes.

JAKE. You're going to have such a great time in Leeds.

WILL. Yeah?

WILL *isn't sure what he should be doing. So he's doing nothing.*

JAKE. I really wanted to do that course.

WILL. Well, it's your reserve, though, so…

WILL *stands. He takes off his T-shirt.*

He folds his arms over his chest.

He watches JAKE *so-so-so carefully.*

JAKE. Yeah.

WILL. If you don't get the grades…

JAKE. Yeah. But don't make it like that…

WILL. No. I –

JAKE. Because it's not. It's just, Cambridge is Cambridge, right? I mean, it just is…

WILL. Part of me hopes you don't get the grades.

JAKE. No.

WILL. Though, if you didn't, I probably wouldn't either, and then you'd be going to Leeds and I'll go to Middlesex and…

JAKE. No. You'll get your…

WILL. You'll definitely get yours.

JAKE. I don't know.

WILL. No. You will.

JAKE. Do you really think so?

WILL. Definitely.

JAKE. I hope so. I mean, I'm working hard enough, so…

WILL. Definitely.

JAKE. Still, three As…

WILL. I know.

JAKE. With my GCSEs –

WILL. Yeah, but you didn't try in GCSE –

JAKE. Yeah. I know.

WILL. Whereas, this time…

JAKE. I read a textbook the other weekend. The whole thing.

WILL. Yeah?

JAKE. You really think I will…? You wouldn't…?

WILL. Definitely.

WILL thinks and then turns around and pulls off his boxer shorts.

He then realises he hasn't got his new boxer shorts ready and looks for his bag.

He sees it.

Beside JAKE's chair.

He thinks about pulling up his boxer shorts again, but dismisses the thought; he cups his bollocks in his hand, and then turns and looks at JAKE. He is still facing forward.

WILL thinks and then lets go of the cup and bravely walks up and picks up his bag as if it's nothing.

The boys brush against each other.

Both stiffen. WILL slightly more openly.

JAKE. Well, whatever…

WILL. You will. And then you'll be Prime Minister. Probably the youngest ever.

JAKE. Blair's forty-three.

WILL starts to pull on his clothes rapidly.

WILL. You'll be…

JAKE. Youngest since Lord Liverpool, who was forty-two when he became Prime Minister in 1812.

WILL. You can do that.

JAKE. Who was the youngest since… William Pitt was twenty-four, when he became – in 1783 –

WILL. Well, maybe not [that] –

> JAKE *starts to laugh,* WILL *laughs too. Neither quite know why.*

> I think you could beat Blair. I mean, that's twenty-five years, and think all the stuff you've achieved by the time you're eighteen.

JAKE. And what will you…?

WILL. I'll be your Chancellor or something…

JAKE. No. You'd need Economics and Maths for that…

WILL. Really? I'm shit at…

JAKE. Yeah. The Civil Servants will walk all over you if you haven't – it's why I wish I did A-level Maths.

WILL. You did Economics.

JAKE. Yes, but Maths…

WILL *(considering).* Maybe you should have done it instead of History?

JAKE. You could be Chief Whip. Thy will be done.

WILL. Yeah?

JAKE. It's a surprisingly… surprisingly influential position.

WILL. Yeah.

JAKE. Other than the big four it's probably the position works closest with the Prime Minister.

WILL. Yeah? Yeah.

JAKE. God. Sorry. Why am I talking like you know nothing about politics? Sorry. Sorry.

WILL. No. I –

JAKE. You know loads about politics. You probably know more than me…

WILL. No.

JAKE. No?

WILL. No.

JAKE *sits back on the floor and resumes cutting out articles.* WILL *watches him.*

Do you read all of them?

JAKE. They're reference mostly. You don't need to read reference. You just need to have it.

WILL. Right.

JAKE. I put them in a huge file and then when something comes up I have them there. For reference. It's like a dictionary of newspaper clippings.

WILL. Great.

JAKE. I forget you haven't been in my room much.

WILL. Not much. We generally just –

JAKE. You know, I'd quite like it if we both ended up at the same [place] –

WILL. Yeah?

JAKE. University.

WILL. Yeah?

JAKE. We could do the first year in halls…

WILL. What [halls]?

JAKE. Student accommodation. Basically it means these huge blocks built by the –

WILL. Oh, I've seen those. Yeah. Halls of residence. I get what you're… Just call them… abbreviate them to 'halls', do they? I don't know much about – accommodation…

JAKE. That's because neither of your parents went to university.

WILL. Yeah. Probably. I mean, I know some stuff…

JAKE. First year in halls, and then we could get a flat or something in our second year.

WILL. Okay. Yeah. That sounds [great].

JAKE. I mean, it's not a problem, your parents having not gone to university.

WILL. No. I know.

JAKE. You're exactly what the Party is all about, frankly. You're the reason I'm pleased Dad couldn't afford to send me to private school.

WILL. Yeah.

JAKE. And sometimes we could go out into Leeds and try and pull or whatever and sometimes we could stay in. And you know, that year abroad thing could be…

WILL. In America.

JAKE. Exactly. Maybe I should reject Cambridge if I get in…

WILL. Yeah?

JAKE. No. Probably –

WILL. No.

Pause.

JAKE. We just got to concentrate on getting that second term – I mean, with this mandate – but still… it could…

WILL. Yeah.

JAKE. But if we concentrate, if we keep moving forward, if we stick to our promises, we could –

WILL. Yeah.

JAKE *moves and wants to clap his hands, but doesn't.*

JAKE. Anyway. Do you want brekkie-breakfast?

WILL. Do you?

JAKE. Liz might be out of the kitchen by now. Depending on whether she thinks it's important to wash before [school] or just do her nails. Is it weird washing after you do your – ?

WILL. I'm not going to [wash] –

JAKE. No time. But breakfast – Dad keeps a good range of cereal in.

WILL. Okay.

JAKE. None of those party packs or… Full-size boxes. Just – a few of them, rather than one. Me and Dad eat plenty of cereal.

WILL. Okay.

JAKE. And I like a range. I like a range of cereal. And there's never enough in a fun-size.

WILL. No. I know what you mean…

JAKE. And we could memorise the new Cabinet together.

WILL. Yeah. Who's Chief Whip?

JAKE. Exactly! I have no idea. It'd be brilliant if both of us knew everything.

WILL. I know.

JAKE. Not just to show Carla or anything…

WILL. I know.

JAKE. I'm never fingering her again anyway, so…

WILL. Yeah…? Yeah.

JAKE. She had too much pubic hair too.

WILL. Yeah?

JAKE. Yeah, I couldn't tell if I was hitting… if I was hitting the right [places] –

WILL. Yeah?

JAKE. I did. But it took me a while.

WILL. Yeah.

> JAKE *makes for the door.*
>
> *And then stops.*
>
> *He turns with a tumescent smile.*

JAKE. Will…

WILL. Yeah.

JAKE. Can you believe it?

WILL. No.

JAKE. We crushed them.

WILL. I know. And I like how it's 'we' too.

JAKE. Of course it's… We leafleted Slough, Ascot and Reading West. Martin Salter. We canvassed where they let us. It's definitely… It's 'we'. It's 'us'.

WILL. Yeah.

JAKE. I'm really… I can't believe how good I feel.

WILL. I know.

JAKE. I feel powerful.

WILL. You are. We are.

JAKE. Like He-Man. 'I – have – the – power.'

WILL (*giggles*). I'll be Man-At-Arms.

JAKE. She-Ra, right right. She-Ra, right.

WILL. The tiger thing. What was the tiger – called?

JAKE. I don't know. I've never watched much kids' TV.

WILL. No.

JAKE. Seven Cabinet Ministers gone. Half their fucking seats. 418 seats.

WILL. It's amazing.

JAKE. I feel like I can do anything.

WILL. You can. You will. I mean, definitely.

JAKE thinks and then moves to hug WILL. They hesitate a moment and then they hug. JAKE's back is towards us, but we see WILL's face really clearly. He's concentrating really hard on not getting an erection.

Then he smells JAKE's hair and can't help himself.

JAKE dislocates.

He looks at WILL for a moment. And then JAKE kisses WILL on the mouth. Just a peck but a significant one at that. They hold for a moment.

As he breaks off, JAKE smiles like he's done WILL a huge favour. And WILL smiles because, well...

JAKE. I knew it was going to happen, but not like this...

WILL tries to digest what just happened.

WILL. No.

He smiles. And then he doesn't. JAKE is watching him so-so carefully, but he's not showing it. WILL knows everything.

JAKE. Such a majority. Such a...

WILL. Yeah. Jake –

JAKE. It's brilliant. It's like everything's new. I'm so excited.

WILL. Yeah? Jake –

JAKE. What?

WILL takes a sniff and then a breath.

He opens his mouth to speak. JAKE turns to look at him.

Spit it out.

WILL says nothing. JAKE laughs.

As the bishop said to the choirboy.

WILL. I – um – come to – come to Leeds with me –

JAKE. What?

WILL thinks how to say it differently; he can't.

WILL. Come to Leeds.

JAKE looks at WILL closely. WILL swallows.

JAKE. I can't. I'd be – betraying – myself.

WILL. Okay. Okay.

Beat. WILL nods. Then nods again. JAKE just keeps looking at him.

Remember I asked, though, won't you?

JAKE turns away – he knows what WILL means.

JAKE. Yeah. Of course.

Beat.

And maybe I won't get the grades so…

WILL. Okay.

JAKE. No. No. I'm pleased you've asked. I could make sure you'd stay good. You'd – (*Like ET.*) be good.

He touches WILL's nose. And then his heart.

(*Like ET.*) Be good. You are good.

Then he smiles.

You're – good.

The two boys stare at each other for a moment more.

JAKE breaks first, with a grin.

My dad told me once there was two clues to getting along in life: never go to a supermarket when you're hungry and never make a decision when you've got an erection. He was drunk. Which I guess is probably another clue – never give your child advice when drunk. I think there's one clue really – enjoy what you've got when you get it and then try and keep it.

We're going to be great.

Mark the moment.

JAKE *grins and exits.* WILL *hesitates a moment, looks around the room and smiles. And then doesn't smile.*

WILL. Yeah.

WILL *exits.*

Slow fade. Black.

The End.

A Nick Hern Book

2nd May 1997 first published in Great Britain as a paperback original in 2009 by Nick Hern Books Limited, 14 Larden Road, London W3 7ST, in association with the Bush Theatre, London

2nd May 1997 copyright © 2009 Jack Thorne

Jack Thorne has asserted his right to be identified as the author of this work

Cover image by aka
Cover design by Ned Hoste, 2H

Typeset by Nick Hern Books
Printed and bound in Great Britain by CPI Antony Rowe, Chippenham, Wiltshire

A CIP catalogue record for this book is available from the British Library

ISBN 978 1 84842 080 9